Fact Cat

THE FIRST WORLD WAR

Izzi Howell

WAYLAND
www.waylandbooks.co.uk

FACT CAT

Get your paws on this fantastic new mega-series from Wayland!

Join our Fact Cat on a journey of fun learning about every subject under the sun!

First published in Great Britain in 2017 by Wayland
Copyright © Hodder and Stoughton Limited, 2017

ISBN: 978 1 5263 0522 0

10 9 8 7 6 5 4 3 2 1

MIX
Paper from responsible sources
FSC® C104740

Wayland
An imprint of Hachette Children's Group
Part of Hodder & Stoughton
Carmelite House
50 Victoria Embankment
London EC4Y oDZ

An Hachette UK Company
www.hachette.co.uk
www.hachettechildrens.co.uk

A catalogue for this title is available from the British Library
Printed and bound in China

Produced for Wayland by
White-Thomson Publishing Ltd
www.wtpub.co.uk

Editor: Izzi Howell
Design: Clare Nicholas
Fact Cat illustrations: Shutterstock/Julien Troneur
Consultant: Karina Philip

Picture and illustration credits:
Alamy: Glasshouse Images 17; Getty: ©Corbis 4, John Parrot/Stocktrek Images 6, Dorling Kindersley 7 and 8; Shutterstock: Everett Historical title page, 9, 10, 11, 12, 13t, 13b, 14, 15, 16, 18 and 19, Bertl123 20, Philip Bird LRPS CPAGB 21; Stefan Chabluk: 5, Wayland Picture Library cover. Should there be any inadvertent omission, please apply to the publisher for rectification.

The author, Izzi Howell, is a writer and editor specialising in children's educational publishing.

The consultant, Karina Philip, is a teacher and a primary literacy consultant with an MA in creative writing.

FACT CAT FACT

There is a question for you to answer on most spreads in this book. You can check your answers on page 24.

CONTENTS

THE FIRST WORLD WAR

The First World War was a war between many countries. Over 30 countries took part in the war. It lasted four years, from 1914 to 1918.

Soldiers in the First World War fought each other on **battlefields**. They used weapons such as **bombs** and **machine guns**.

The First World War was about land and power. At the beginning of the war, the United Kingdom, France and Russia fought against Germany and **Austria-Hungary**. Later, more countries joined in.

UNITED KINGDOM

BELGIUM

GERMANY

RUSSIA

FRANCE

AUSTRIA-HUNGARY

This map shows the countries that fought against each other at the beginning of the war. The red countries were called the **Central Powers**. The yellow countries were called the **Allies**.

FACT CAT **FACT**

Around 8.5 **million** soldiers died in the First World War.

OFF TO WAR

The First World War began on 28 July 1914.
Over a million men joined the British army.
They wanted to fight for their country.
Everyone thought that the war would end quickly.

This poster was made to encourage men to join the British army.

British soldiers had to bring the **equipment** they needed for battle. They wore uniforms and carried **bayonets**.

helmet

jacket

bayonet

British soldiers wore boots, thick green wool trousers and jacket and a metal helmet. Which part of the uniform was called the 'puttees'?

trousers

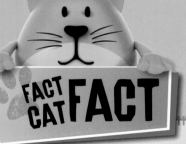

FACT CAT **FACT**

British soldiers also had to bring soap, a towel and a knife and fork!

BATTLEFIELDS

Many battles in the First World War took place in France and Belgium. Soldiers fought from **trenches** dug into the ground. The battlefields became muddy after weeks of fighting and rain.

No Man's Land

FIRING LINE H.Q.

The land between the trenches was called **No Man's Land**. Soldiers fired across No Man's Land at the enemy trenches.

These soldiers are about to 'go over the top' (come out of a trench to cross No Man's Land). Going over the top was terrifying. The soldiers knew that they might die.

Sometimes, soldiers crossed No Man's Land to try to **capture** enemy trenches. Crossing No Man's Land was very dangerous. The enemy used guns, bombs and **poison gas** to stop the soldiers.

FACT CAT FACT

On 25 December 1914, a few enemy soldiers stopped fighting. They sang carols, gave each other presents and played football in No Man's Land. Which festival were they celebrating?

LIFE IN THE TRENCHES

Soldiers also lived in the trenches. They slept, ate and waited for battle.

These German soldiers are passing time in the trenches by reading, sleeping and talking to each other.

It was very uncomfortable in the trenches. Soldiers were usually cold, wet and dirty. They had **lice** in their clothes and hair, because they couldn't clean themselves.

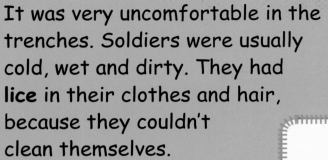

Injured soldiers stayed in the trenches if they could still fight. If they were badly hurt, they were taken to hospital.

WEAPONS

Poison gas was one of the most dangerous weapons. The gas travelled through the air. The soldiers couldn't run away from it. They died when they breathed in the gas.

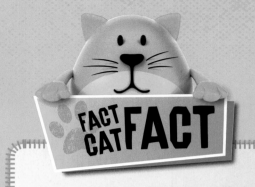

Some soldiers didn't die from poison gas attacks. However, the gas often damaged their eyes, **lungs** and skin.

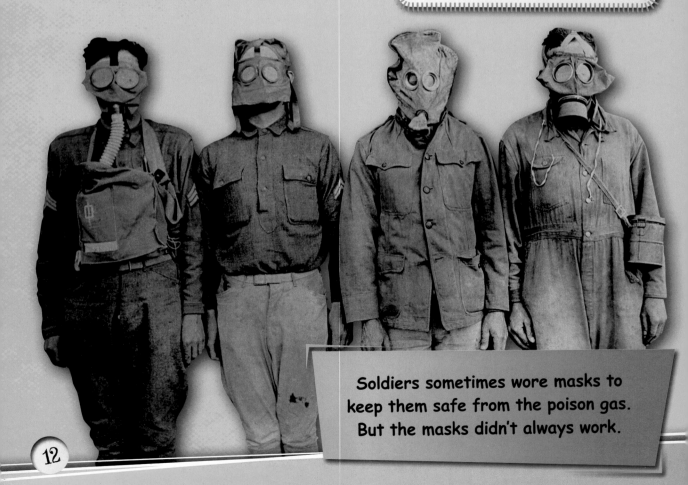

Soldiers sometimes wore masks to keep them safe from the poison gas. But the masks didn't always work.

Tanks protected soldiers from bullets and bombs. This meant that they could move closer to the enemy without getting hurt.

Soldiers in the First World War fought with new weapons, such as machine guns and tanks. These weapons hadn't been used in wars before.

The machine guns used in the First World War could shoot lots of bullets very quickly.

SEA AND SKY

Some First World War battles took place at sea. Both sides had large war ships. German **submarines** shot **torpedoes** at ships travelling to Britain.

In the Battle of Jutland, around 250 British and German war ships attacked each other with guns and torpedoes.

torpedo

Aeroplanes were used as a weapon for the first time in the First World War. Pilots **spied** on the enemy's **location** and dropped bombs.

French aeroplane

Aeroplane pilots fought each other in the air. They shot machine guns at each other. These fights were called dogfights.

German aeroplane

FACT CAT FACT

The first aeroplane flight took place in 1903, only eleven years before the start of the First World War! What were the names of the brothers who designed and flew the world's first aeroplane?

AT HOME

The First World War changed everyday life for people away from the fighting. Women had to work in factories and on farms. Before the war, these were usually men's jobs.

This woman is making weapons in a factory in the USA.

There was less food for people at home. Ships bringing food to Britain were destroyed during sea battles. Lots of food had to be sent to soldiers in other countries.

People at home in Britain were told not to waste bread.

DON'T WASTE BREAD!

SAVE TWO SLICES EVERY DAY and Defeat the 'U' Boat

FACT CAT FACT

There wasn't enough flour to make bread in Britain during the First World War. Instead, people made bread from potatoes and turnips!

THE WAR ENDS

In 1917, the USA joined the war. They fought on the same side as the Allies. They brought many soldiers and weapons. The Allies were now much stronger than the Central Powers.

US soldiers fought with Allied soldiers on the battlefields. Which country's flag is shown in this photo?

People found out that the war had ended by reading newspapers and listening to the radio.

FACT CAT FACT

On 11 November 1918, Germany **surrendered** and the war finished. People were happy that the First World War had ended. However, it was a sad time as so many soldiers had been injured or killed.

The First World War ended at 11 a.m. on the 11 November 1918. November is the eleventh month of the year.

REMEMBERING THE WAR

People wanted to remember the First World War after it finished. They didn't want another world war to happen ever again. However, the Second World War started 21 years later in 1939.

War memorials were built in many towns to pay respect to the soldiers that died in battle. This is the Guards War Memorial in London.

THIS MEMORIAL ALSO COMMEMORATES ALL THOSE MEMBERS OF THE HOUSEHOLD DIVISION WHO DIED IN THE SECOND WORLD WAR AND IN THE SERVICE OF THEIR COUNTRY SINCE 1918

Every year on 11 November, we remember people who died in the First World War and other wars. This day is known as **Remembrance Day**.

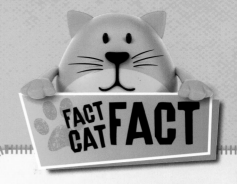

FACT CAT FACT

People wear **poppies** to celebrate Remembrance Day because of a famous poem, 'In Flanders Fields ', by Lieutenant Colonel John McCrae. In the poem, the writer describes how poppies grew on the First World War battlefields during the war.

People lay **wreaths** of poppies on war memorials on Remembrance Sunday. When is Remembrance Sunday?

QUIZ

Try to answer the questions below. Look back through the book to help you. Check your answers on page 24.

1 The UK, France and Russia were called the Allies. True or not true?

a) true

b) not true

2 In which country did many battles take place?

a) Belgium

b) the UK

c) the USA

3 No Man's Land was between the trenches. True or not true?

a) true

b) not true

4 Dogfights were battles between ships. True or not true?

a) true

b) not true

5 What did women do during the war?

a) fight in the army

b) sail ships

c) work in factories and on farms

6 When is Remembrance Day?

a) 1 November

b) 11 November

c) 11 December

GLOSSARY

Allies the armies of Britain, France, Russia and later, the USA, that fought on the same side in the First World War

Austria-Hungary In the past, this was an empire ruled by one person, but today it is divided into many countries, such as Austria, Hungary and the Czech Republic.

battlefield a place where a battle is fought

bayonet a gun with a knife on the end

bomb a weapon that will explode

capture to take control of an area

Central Powers the armies of Germany, Austria-Hungary and other countries that fought on the same side in the First World War

encourage to make someone want to do something

equipment the objects that are needed to do something

injured hurt

lice very small insects that live on people's hair and skin and bite them

location where someone or something is

lungs the body part with which we breathe

machine gun a weapon that quickly fires many bullets

million one thousand thousand (1,000,000)

No Man's Land an area of land between the trenches that no-one controls

poison gas gas that will hurt or kill you if you breathe it in

poppy a red flower that grew on the battlefields of the First World War

Remembrance Day an event on 11 November in which people remember and pay respect to those who died in wars throughout history

spy to secretly try to get information

submarine a boat that travels under water

surrender to stop fighting and say that you have lost

torpedo an underwater bomb that is fired from a ship

trench a long narrow hole dug into the ground

USA the United States of America

wreath a large ring of leaves and flowers twisted together

INDEX

ANSWERS

Pages 4–20

Page 7: The strips of fabric around the lower legs. Puttees is the Hindi word for bandage.

Page 9: Christmas

Page 15: The Wright Brothers

Page 18: The USA's

Page 21: The closest Sunday to Remembrance Day.

Quiz answers

1   true

2   a - Belgium

3   true

4   not true – they were battles between aeroplanes.

5   c – work in factories and on farms

6   b – 11 November

OTHER TITLES IN THE FACT CAT SERIES...

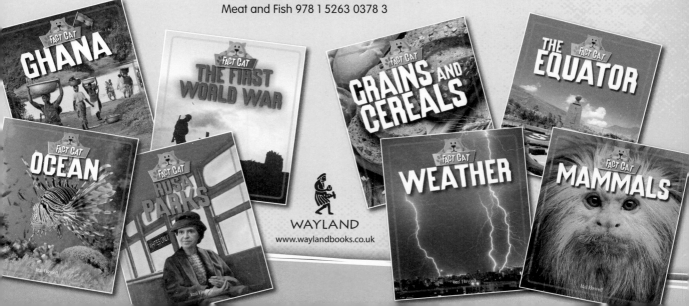

WAYLAND
www.waylandbooks.co.uk